LET'S INVESTIGATE
Solids

LET'S INVESTIGATE
Solids

By Marion Smoothey

Illustrated by Ted Evans

MARSHALL CAVENDISH
NEW YORK · LONDON · TORONTO · SYDNEY

Library Edition Published 1993

© Marshall Cavendish Corporation 1993

Published by Marshall Cavendish Corporation
2415 Jerusalem Avenue
PO Box 587
North Bellmore
New York 11710

Series created by Graham Beehag Book Design

Library of Congress Cataloging-in-Publication Data

Smoothey, Marion, 1943-
    Solids / by Marion Smoothey; illustrated by Ted Evans.
       p. cm.. -- (Let's Investigate)
    Includes index.
    Summary: Explores the world of solid shapes and how they can be created, measured, and used in various activities.
    ISBN 1-85435-469-8 ISBN 1-85435-463-9 (set)
    1. Geometry, Solid -- Juvenile literature.
    [1. Shape. 2. Geometry, Solid.]
    I. Evans, Ted ill. II. Title. III. Series:
    Smoothey, Marion, 1943- Let's Investigate.
    QA457.S88 1993   92-38220
    516.23---dc20   CIP
                                         AC

Printed in Malaysia by Times Offset (M) SDN BHD
Bound in the United States

Contents

This book will show you many things to make and do. Some of them you will be able to do in your head, but often you will need to make a model to solve a problem.

You will need a good supply of fairly heavy graph paper or thin cardboard. For most of the models, you will need $\frac{1}{2}''$ squares. Sometimes you will need a grid of triangles. You can copy the one at the back of the book.

 You will also need scissors, a ruler, a compass, a protractor, a sharp pencil, tape and some glue. The glue that comes in a stick is the easiest to work with.

When you have to fold along a dotted line, it is a good idea to score the line first with a ruler and scissors blade.

Have fun!

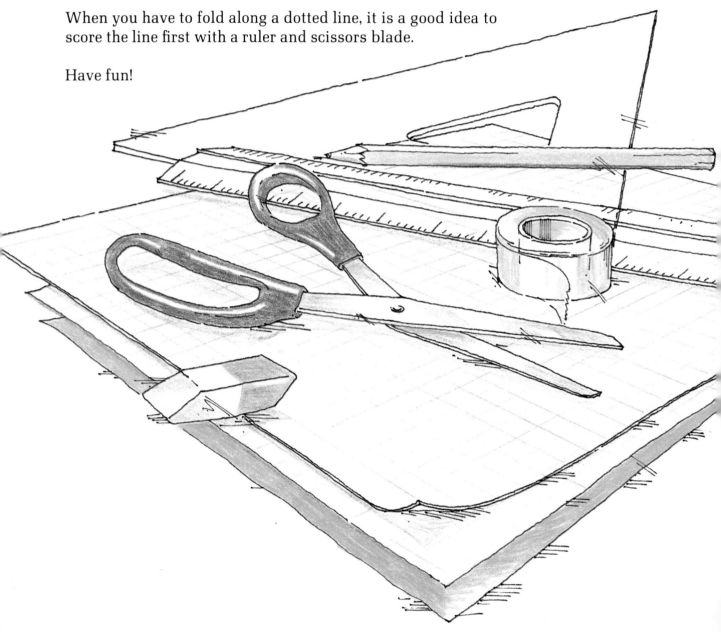

Open Boxes

You need thick paper or thin cardboard with squares printed on it, pencil, ruler, scissors and tape. If you don't have graph paper, you need a **set square.**

Making a set square

You can make a set square by making two folds in a piece of tablet paper or cardboard. It does not need to have square corners.

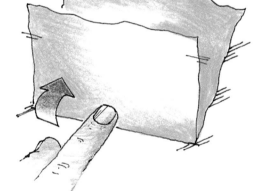

1. Make a fold approximately across the middle of the piece of paper.

2. Place the two ends of the fold together. Make a second fold. Make sure that the two edges of the original fold are exactly on top of each other. The angle at the corner of the two folds will then be a **right angle**.

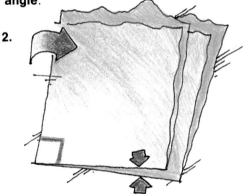

Open box puzzles

Cut out a $4\frac{1}{2}''$ square. It is important to make it exactly square. If your paper or cardboard does not have squares printed on it, use a set square to check.

● **1.** Without cutting, make an open box from the square. An open box is a box without a top.

● **2.** Using scissors, but without cutting any paper off the square, make an open box.

● **3.** Make an open box from the square by cutting off parts of it.

Answers to open box puzzles

1. Fold into nine $1\frac{1}{2}$" squares as shown.

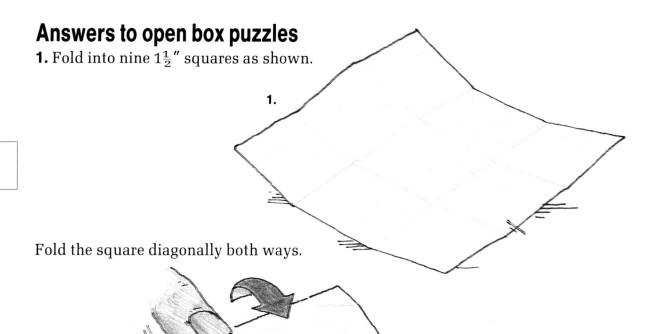

1.

Fold the square diagonally both ways.

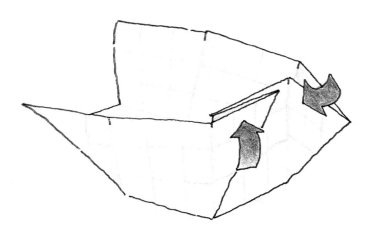

Fold up from the middle to make the box. Fasten with tape.

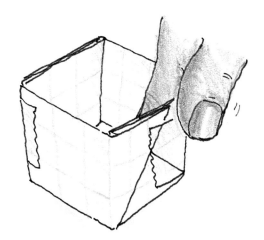

You may need to score along the fold lines with the point of a scissors blade and a ruler to get a sharp crease. (See page 6.)

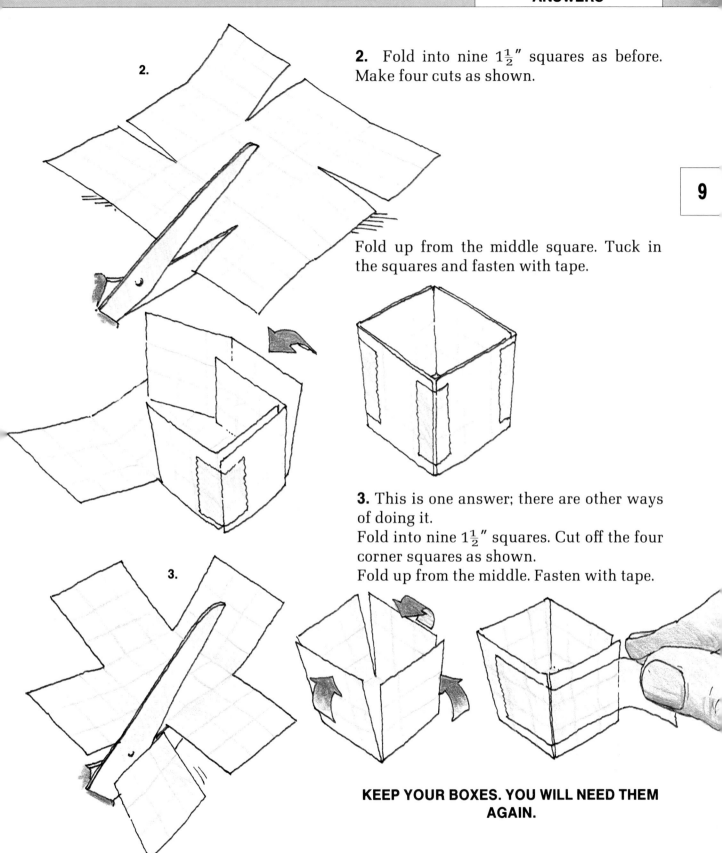

2. Fold into nine $1\frac{1}{2}''$ squares as before. Make four cuts as shown.

Fold up from the middle square. Tuck in the squares and fasten with tape.

3. This is one answer; there are other ways of doing it.
Fold into nine $1\frac{1}{2}''$ squares. Cut off the four corner squares as shown.
Fold up from the middle. Fasten with tape.

KEEP YOUR BOXES. YOU WILL NEED THEM AGAIN.

Pentominoes

The shape used to make the third open box is called a **pentomino**. A pentomino is five squares joined together with whole sides touching.

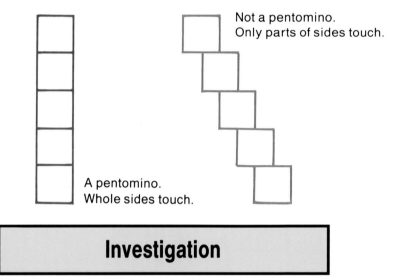

Not a pentomino.
Only parts of sides touch.

A pentomino.
Whole sides touch.

Investigation

● How many *different* pentominoes can you find that will fold up to make an open box?

Here are different ways of looking at the *same* pentomino.

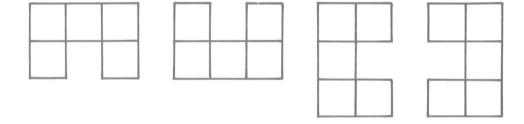

Faces, Edges and Vertices

Look carefully at one of your open boxes. It has **faces.**

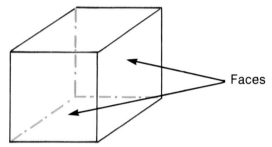

Faces

● **1.** How many faces does your box have?
● **2.** What shape are they?

Each face on your box has four **edges.**

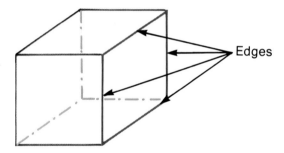

Edges

● **3.** How many edges does your box have?

It also has **vertices** where the edges meet.

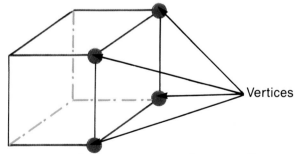

Vertices

4. How many edges meet at each **vertex?**
5. How many vertices are there on the box?

Cubes

A closed box with square faces is a cube. It does not matter whether it is solid or hollow; it is still a cube.

A closed box with faces that are **rectangles** is a **cuboid**. A cube is a special cuboid, just as a square is a special rectangle. A cube is a cuboid with six square faces. A square is a rectangle with four equal sides.

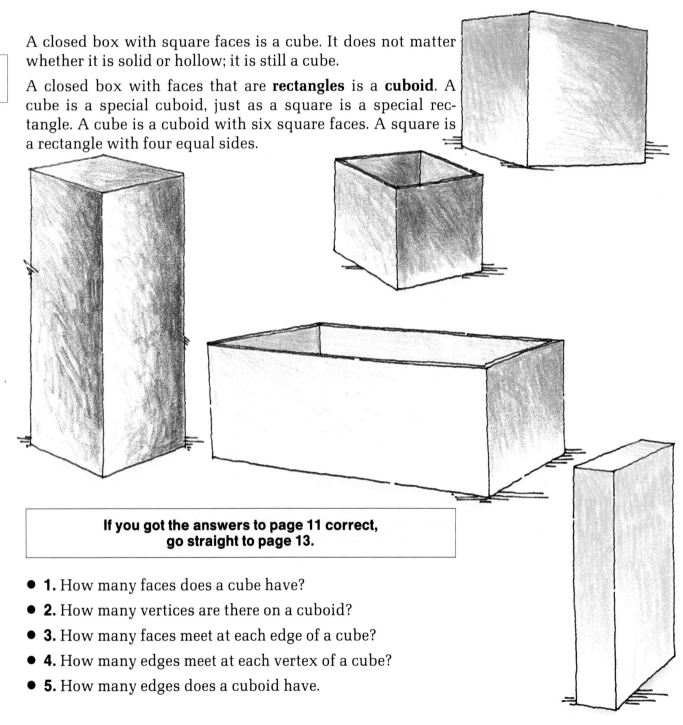

**If you got the answers to page 11 correct,
go straight to page 13.**

- **1.** How many faces does a cube have?
- **2.** How many vertices are there on a cuboid?
- **3.** How many faces meet at each edge of a cube?
- **4.** How many edges meet at each vertex of a cube?
- **5.** How many edges does a cuboid have.

Nets

A flat shape that can be folded to form a three-dimensional solid is called a **net**.

When you cut out a net to make a solid, it is a good idea to put a tab on each alternate side. This makes it easy to glue the sides together on the inside. The finished solid will look neater than if you use tape. If you have more tabs than you need, just cut off the extra ones.

13

Investigation

The net of an open box is a pentomino. The net of a cube is a **hexomino** - six squares joined by complete edges.

● **1.** How many different nets are there for a cube?

Challenge

● **2.** What solid will this net make?

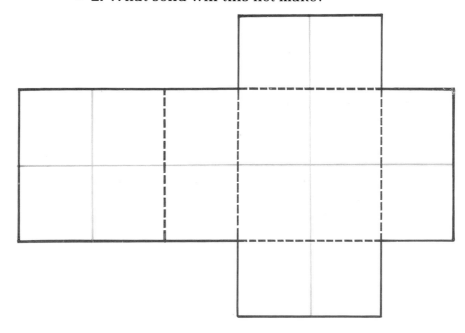

Answers to page 10

Here are the eight pentominoes that will make an open box.

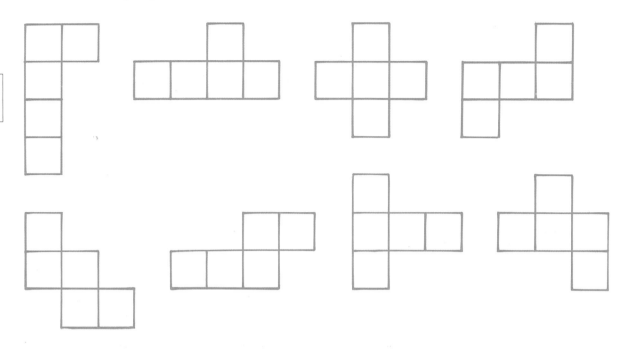

There are the four pentominoes that will not make an open box.

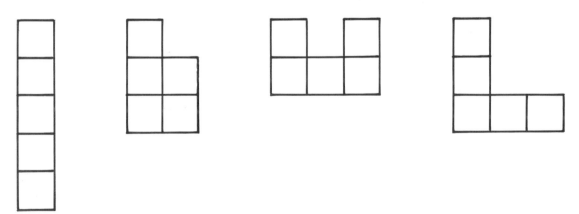

All other pentominoes are **reflections** or **rotations** of these twelve.

Funny Face Boxes

● Ben wants to make an open box with a funny face on the bottom. Which of these nets will work?

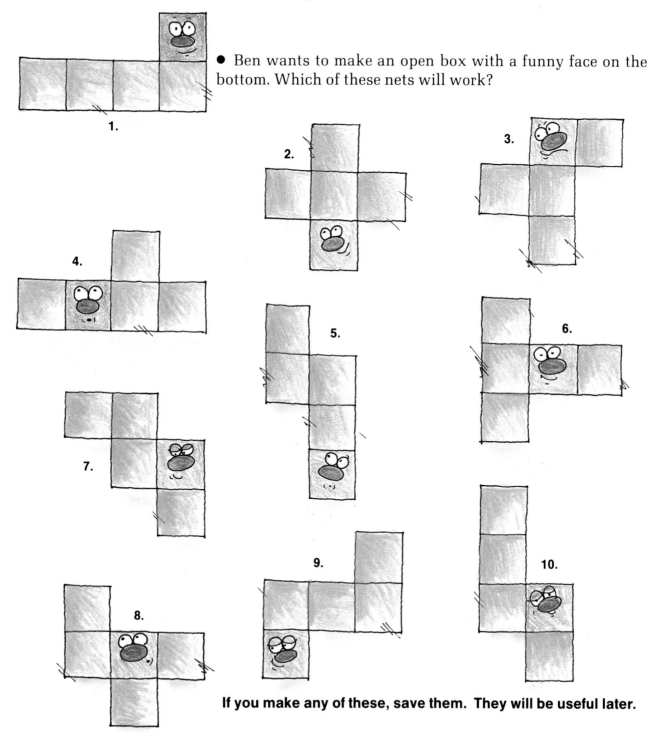

If you make any of these, save them. They will be useful later.

Answers to page 13

1. These are the eleven nets for a cube.

16

All other nets are **reflections** or **rotations** of these.

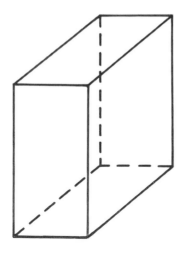

● **2.** The net makes a cuboid. If you make two of the nets and put them together, what will they make?

Half Cubes

There are many ways of cutting a cube into two halves – remember that halves must be equal.

● **1.** See if you can make the net for these two halves.

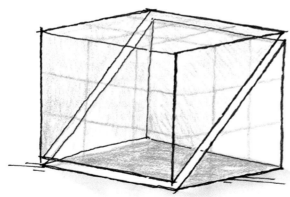

● **2.** These two solids fit together to make a cube. Try to make them.

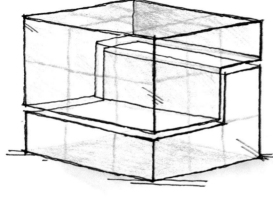

● **3.** The solids are not half cubes – why not?

Prisms

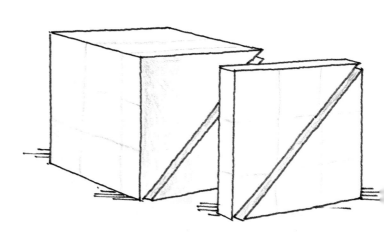

The solids you were asked to make on page 17 are **prisms**. Wherever you cut across them at right angles to the ends, you get the same shape as the ends.

A wedge of cheese and a hexagonal pencil are both prisms.

● **1.** Are cuboids prisms?

Cylinders

Cylinders are prisms that have circular ends. A coin, a can, a length of wire and a pencil can all be cylinders.

18

● **2.** The net of a cylinder has three pieces. What are the names of the pieces?

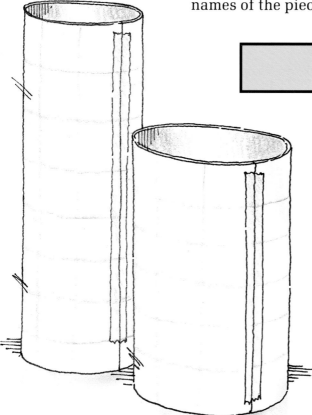

Investigation

◇ Cut two 8″ by 6″ rectangles from thin cardboard. Roll up the cardboard and fasten with tape to make two tubes, one that is 8″ tall and one that is 6″ tall.

◇ Stand one of the tubes upright, with the bottom resting on a flat surface. Fill it with building blocks, sugar cubes, marbles, candies or any similar objects that are all the same size. Count and record how many of the objects it takes to fill the tube.

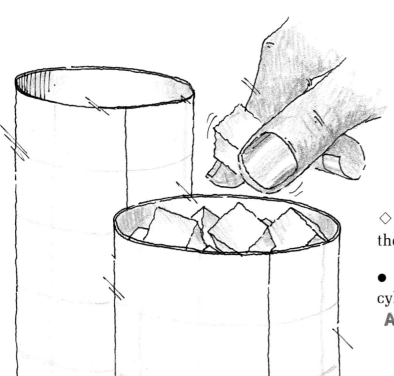

◇ Repeat with the same objects using the second tube.

● Which holds more, a short fat cylinder or a tall thin one?

Answers to page 17

2. If you join two of the cuboids, they make a cube.

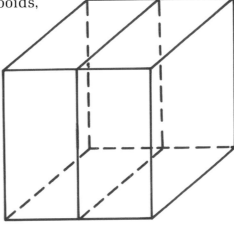

Half Cubes

1. You need two nets like this for the half cube.

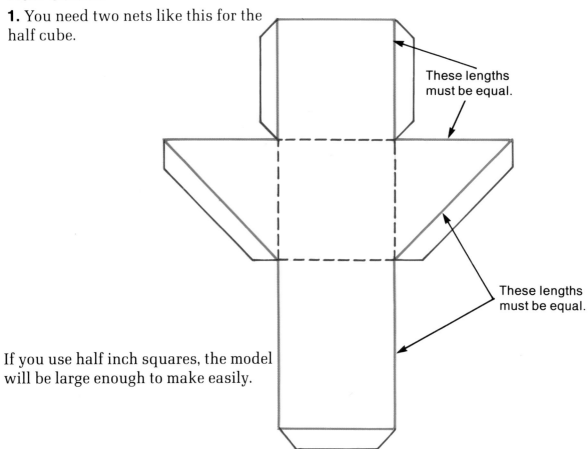

These lengths must be equal.

These lengths must be equal.

If you use half inch squares, the model will be large enough to make easily.

2. Here are the two nets you need.

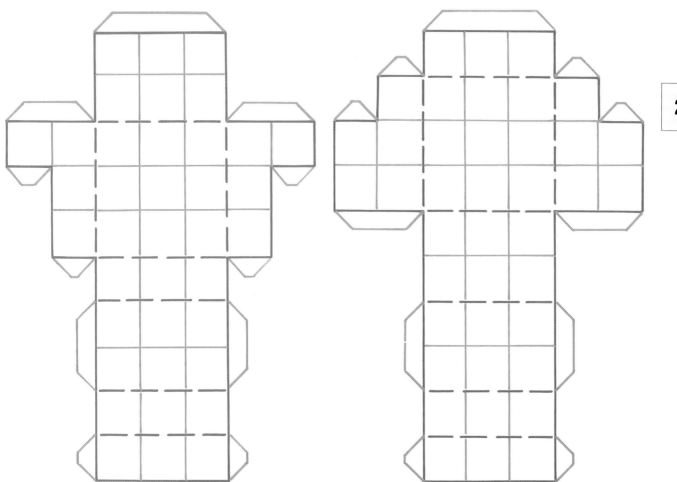

Half inch squares are a good size to use.

3. The prisms are not half cubes because one is bigger than the other. You can tell this by counting the squares in each net.

A Squashed Cuboid

Try to make a net for this solid.

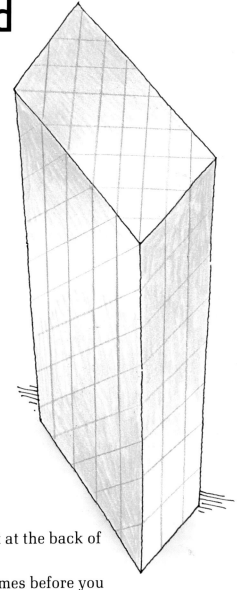

Some hints

What shape are all the faces?

Which faces are the same?

How many faces are there?

Which edges have to match?

Use triangular dotted paper. There is a sheet at the back of the book which you can copy.

You will probably need to try two or three times before you get it quite right.

Drawing Cubes

It is easy to draw cubes if you use triangular dotted paper. There are two ways of looking at triangular dotted paper. If you join four dots to make a **rhombus**, you can see the difference.

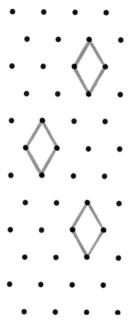

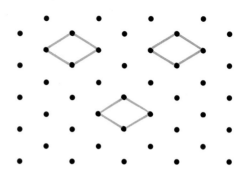

To draw a cube, use the dotted paper this way around.

Begin by joining four dots to make the top of the cube. Then join each corner to the next dot down from it to make the sides of the cube. Draw in the bottom of the cube. Shade the side faces.

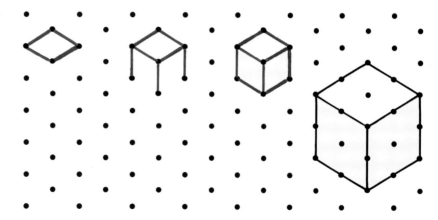

Challenge

Draw the results of each of these arrangements of cubes when joined together.

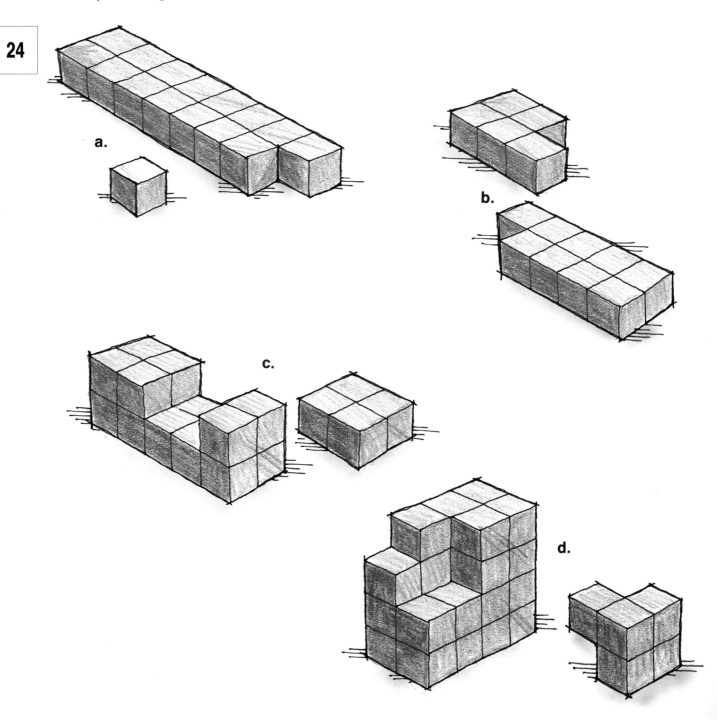

a.

b.

c.

d.

Stacking Cubes

Samantha's puzzle

Samantha Supersmart, the child prodigy, is experimenting with her building blocks. She wants to know how many ways there are of stacking five of them.

Here are two ways of stacking the blocks. One is five stories high: the other is four stories.

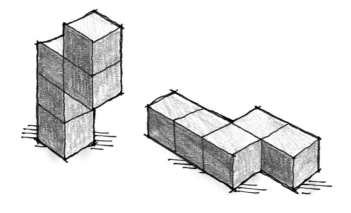

The blocks have to be stacked so that every block touches the whole face of another block and so that they do not fall over. This arrangement does not work as four stories although it does as one story.

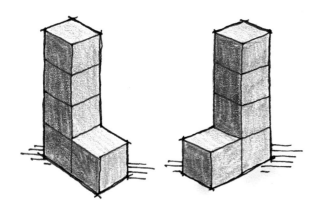

Reflections and **rotations** of the same story count as one way only.

Hints for solving Samantha's problem

It is often a good idea to start with small numbers and work up.

Record your results. One way is to draw the arrangements on triangular dotted paper. If you cannot do this, make the arrangements with blocks, sugar cubes or any other cubes you can find.

See if there is a pattern in your results. If there is, it can help you to check your results or predict the results for larger numbers.

Try to have a system for working through all the possible arrangements so that you do not miss any. It is a good idea to start with all the ways of making four stories, then three and so on.

Evan's puzzle

Evan Plank, the woodworker, wants to make a set of wooden cubes which can be placed together to form four different **cuboids**.

At the moment he can only make one cuboid from the number of cubes which he has made. He has one more cube to make to complete his set.

● How many cubes has he made so far?

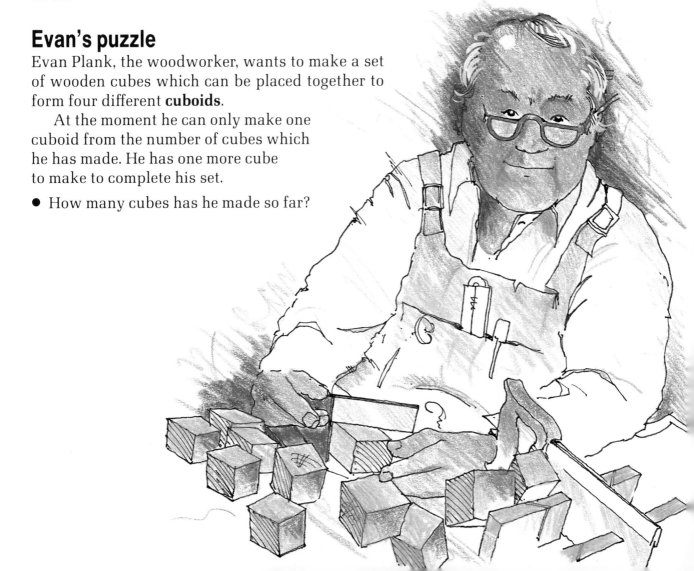

Answer to page 22

You need a net similar to this.

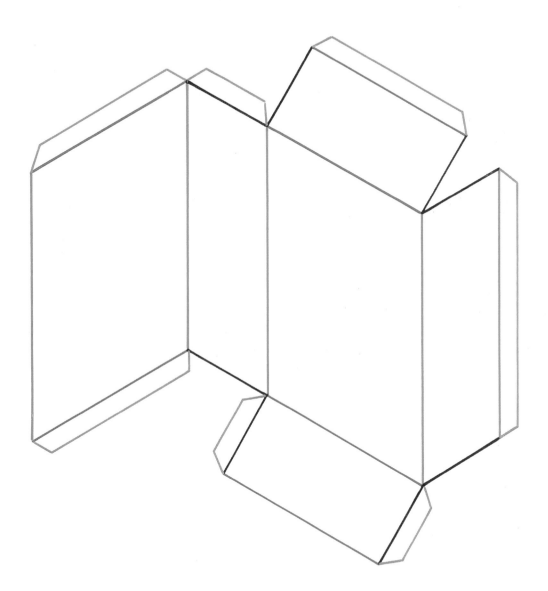

The edges marked in red, blue and green are sets which must be the same length.

The faces are all **parallelograms**.

Cube Puzzle

28

Make these groups of cubes. You can either make your own cubes from nets or use plastic interlocking cubes.

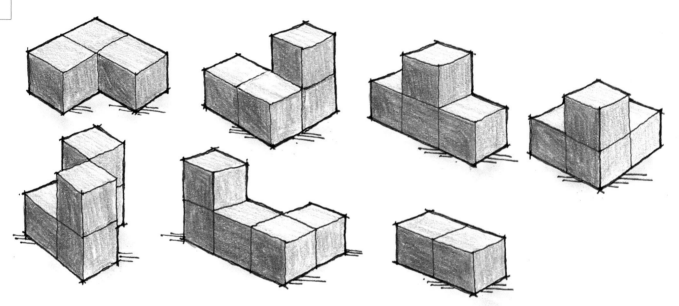

Join them together to make one large cube.

● What size will it be?

Answers to page 24

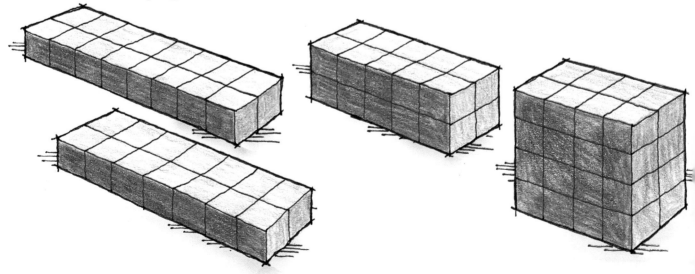

The Rhombic Dodecahedron

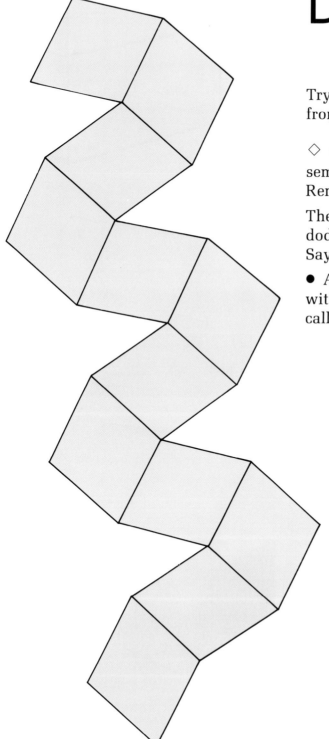

Try to imagine what the solid made from this net looks like.

◇ Copy the net, cut it out and assemble it to see if your idea was right. Remember to put tabs on.

The solid is called a rhombic dodecahedron.
Say "*rombic doh-dec-a-hee-dron.*"

● A **dodecahedron** is a **polyhedron** with twelve faces. Why is this one called **rhombic**?

Polyhedra

Solids with flat faces and straight edges are called polyhedra. This is from two Greek words which mean "many-faced."

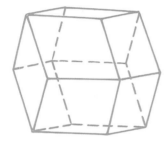

"Dodec" means twelve, so the rhombic dodecahedron you have just made from the net on page 29 is a polyhedron with twelve faces which are **rhombuses.**

Regular polyhedra

Polyhedra with all their faces, edges and vertices the same are called regular. The cube is a regular polyhedron. The squashed cuboid you made on page 22 is not regular. Not all its faces, vertices and edges are the same.

● Is the rhombic dodecahedron a regular polyhedron?

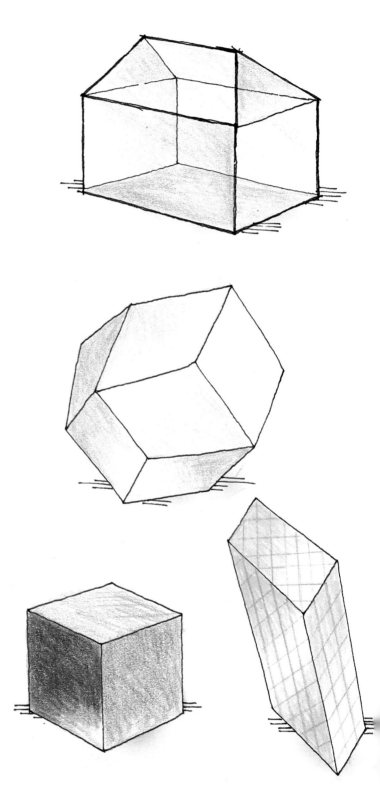

Solving Samantha's puzzle

Here are the ways of stacking four blocks.

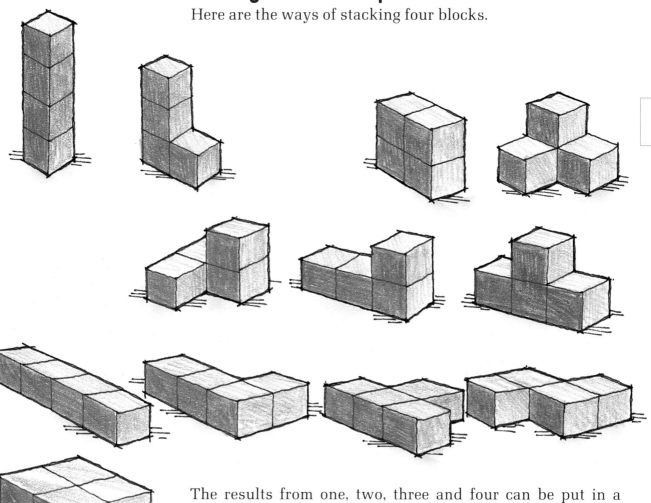

The results from one, two, three and four can be put in a table like this.

Number of cubes	1 story	2 stories	3 stories	4 stories
1	1			
2	1	1		
3	2	1	1	
4	5	5	1	1

There is a pattern of 1's in the last two columns of each row (except the first row which has only one column). This helps you to check for rotations and reflections. Apart from this, the table does not help you very much in this case.

The Platonic Solids

The ancient Greek philosopher Plato discovered that there are five regular polyhedra.

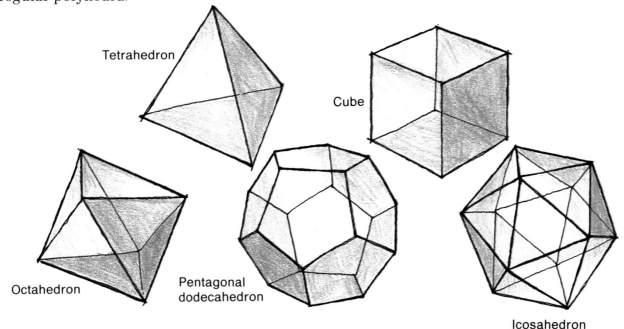

Tetrahedron

Cube

Octahedron

Pentagonal dodecahedron

Icosahedron

These are sometimes called the Platonic solids. It can be proven that there are no other regular **convex** polyhedra.

Convex polyhedra

If two points can be marked on a polyhedron so that the line joining them does not lie completely inside the polyhedron, then the polyhedron is not convex.

The followers of the Ancient Greek mathematician, Pythagoras, believed that the five regular polyhedra had magical powers. They thought that the tetrahedron was connected to fire, the cube to earth, the icosahedron to water, the octahedron to air and the pentagonal dodecahedron to the universe.

Each of the five Platonic solids will fit exactly into a sphere so that sphere touches every **vertex**.

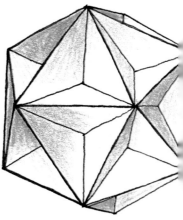

The big dodecahedron

The Sphere

A sphere is a perfect ball. The distance from the center to any point on the surface is always the same.

33

- **1.** How many faces does a sphere have?
- **2.** How many edges?
- **3.** How many vertices?
- **4.** What do you notice about the cross sections?
- **5.** Is a sphere a polyhedron?

Answers to the cube puzzle

There are twenty-seven small cubes. The large cube is $3 \times 3 \times 3$.

● If the large cube was painted red, how many small cubes would have:

   a) three faces painted red
   b) two faces painted red
   c) one face painted red
   d) no faces painted red?

Braiding Solids

A cube

Make a copy of this net on half inch squares.

Cut along the red lines. Fold away from you along the blue dotted lines. Fold **B** over. **A**, **D** over **C**. **F** over **E**, **H** over **G** and so on. When you are left with the flap, tuck it into the slit formed by the overlap of other squares.

● Which squares need to be colored to make a colored cube?

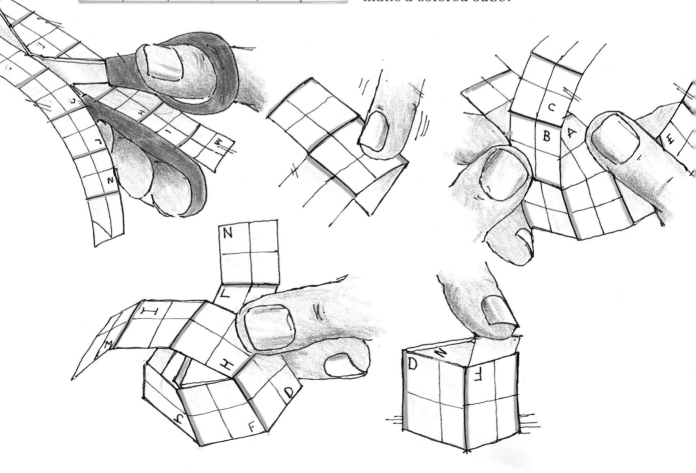

A regular tetrahedron

Use triangular dotted paper to copy this net. Cut out your net. Fold away from you along the blue dotted lines.

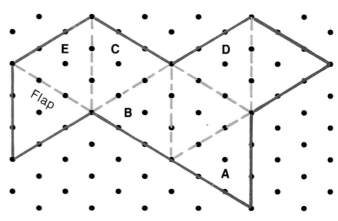

Fold **B** over **A**, **C** over **D**, fold back **E** and tuck in the flap.

You have made a **regular tetrahedron**.

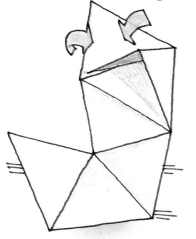

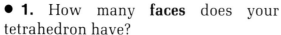

- **1.** How many **faces** does your tetrahedron have?

- **2.** What shape are they?

- **3.** How many **edges** does it have?

- **4.** How many **vertices**?

- **5.** How many edges meet at each vertex?

- **6.** If Albert Ant started at any vertex, could he walk along each edge without going over any edge more than once?

Painting Cubes

Cubes can be joined together to make larger cubes.

● **1.** What is the smallest number of cubes that can be joined together to make a larger cube?

Investigation

If the faces of the larger cubes are painted, only some of the faces of the small cubes are painted. Some will have three faces painted, some two, some one and some no faces painted.

Answer to page 34

The cube you made on page 28 would have eight small cubes with three faces painted, twelve with two faces painted, six with one face painted and, right in the middle, one unpainted cube.

● **2.** What are the results for a $4 \times 4 \times 4$ cube and a $5 \times 5 \times 5$ cube?

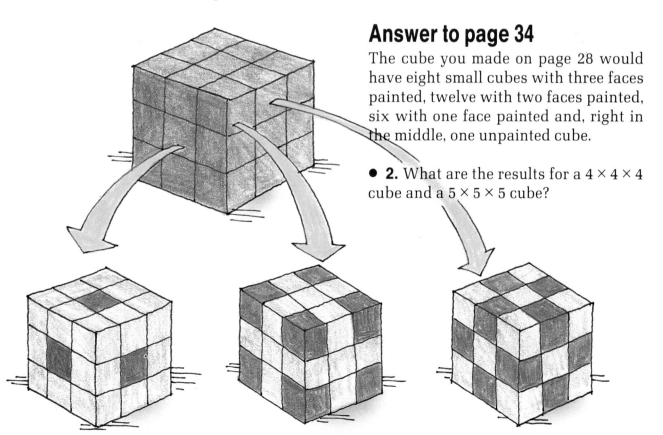

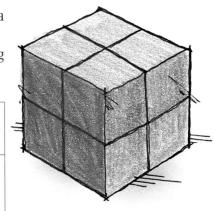

We can arrange the results for different sized cubes in a table.

A 2^3 (2 to the power of 3) cube is a short way of describing a cube made from $2 \times 2 \times 2$ small cubes.

Size of cube	Painted faces				Total small cubes
	3	2	1	0	
3^3	8	12	6	1	27
4^3	8	24	24	8	64
5^3	8	36	54	27	125

Look for patterns in the numbers in the table. Think about **factors** and **powers**.

Use the pattern in the table to tell you how many of each sort of cube there will be in a $100 \times 100 \times 100$ cube.

Answer to Evan's puzzle

He has made eleven cubes so far. He can make only an $11 \times 1 \times 1$ cuboid.

These are the cuboids he can make when he has twelve cubes.

Hidden Faces

If one cube stands on a surface, one face is hidden.

● **1.** If two cubes stand on a surface touching side by side, how many faces are hidden?

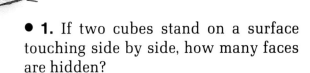

● **2.** Make up a rule for working out how many faces will be hidden for any number of cubes, side by side on a surface.

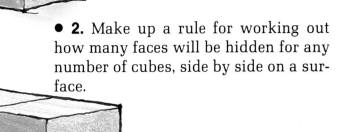

One way to find the rule is to build up a table of results and look for a pattern, but there are other ways of thinking it out.

● **3.** How many faces are hidden when twenty cubes stand side by side on a surface?

Pyramids

Pyramids are polyhedra that have triangular faces that meet at a point.

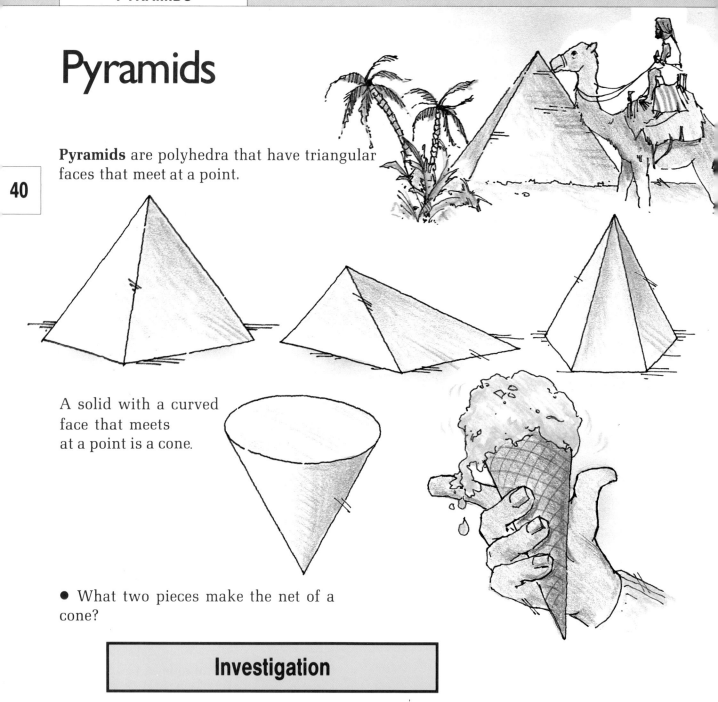

A solid with a curved face that meets at a point is a cone.

● What two pieces make the net of a cone?

Investigation

● **1.** How many ways are there of joining together edge to edge four **equilateral** triangles?

Use triangular dotted paper to record your results.

● **2.** Which of the ways are also nets for a **regular tetrahedron**?

Challenge

A tetrahedron is one kind of pyramid. Design a net for a square based pyramid with four **congruent** triangular faces.

- What shape will the fifth face be?

Octahedra

◇ Make two copies of the net for a square based pyramid. Cut them out and make the pyramids. Fasten the pyramids together by their square bases. You should have a solid like this. It is called an **octahedron**.

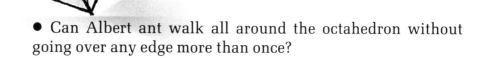

- Can Albert ant walk all around the octahedron without going over any edge more than once?

Net for square-based pyramid

You probably made a net similar to this.

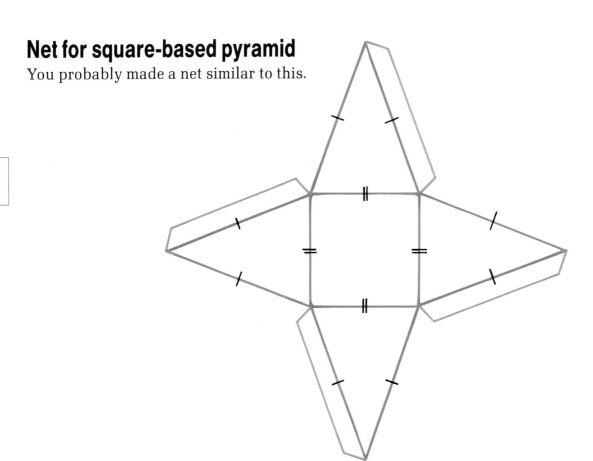

- **1.** What kind of triangles are the ones in the net above?
- **2.** What other kind of triangles can you use for this net?

Right pyramids

The pyramid with four **congruent** triangular faces is called a right pyramid because a line drawn from its point to the center of the base forms a **right angle**.

- **3.** How do you alter the net to make a non-right or slant pyramid?

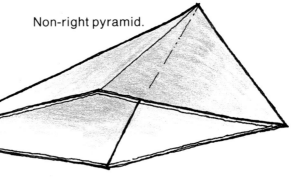

Non-right pyramid.

There is another way of drawing the net for a square based pyramid.

Suppose you want to make the pyramid without the base, like the open boxes at the beginning of the book.

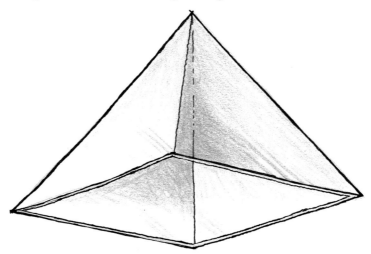

● **1.** How can you make a net for this?

● **2.** How can you adapt the new net to make it a net for a square based pyramid with a base?

● **3.** How many faces are there on a **regular octahedron**?

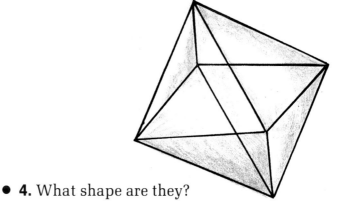

● **4.** What shape are they?

● **5.** Design a net for a regular octahedron.

Investigation

● How many different nets are there for a regular octahedron?

Answers to page 40

These are the two shapes for the net for a cone.

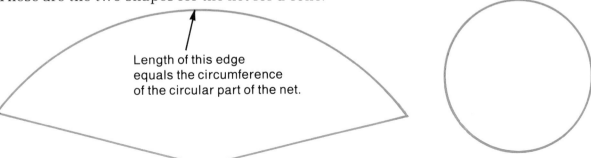

Length of this edge
equals the circumference
of the circular part of the net.

44

1. There are three different ways of joining four equilateral triangles edge to edge.

 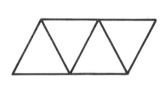 

2. The first two ways are nets for a regular tetrahedron.

Puzzle

● What is the smallest square hole you can cut in a piece of cardboard to allow this regular tetrahedron to pass through it?

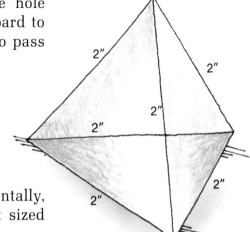

If you cannot work it out mentally, make a model and try different sized holes.

Deltahedra

Investigation

• **Deltahedra** are polyhedra whose faces are all equilateral triangles. How many different **convex** deltahedra can you draw or make?

A way of making the skeletons of polyhedra is to use drinking straws joined together with pipe cleaners.

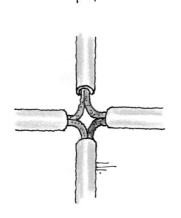

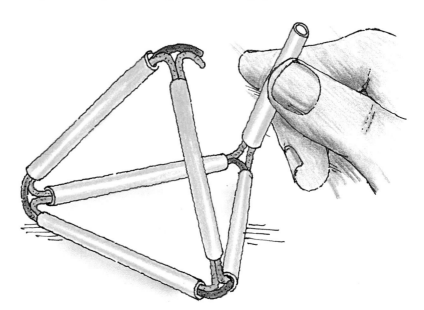

Cut all the pieces of straw to the same length to make deltahedra.

• What happens when you join six equilateral triangles together so that they meet at a point?

Dissections

To dissect something means to cut it.

46

Dissections of a tetrahedron

◇ **1.** Make two copies of this net on triangular dotted paper.
Cut them out and assemble them.

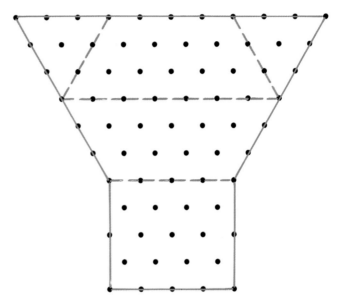

◇ Join the pair of solids to make a **regular tetrahedron**.

◇ **2.** Make four copies of this net. Assemble the solids. Join them to make a tetrahedron.

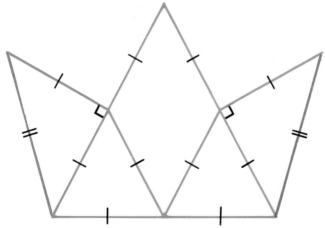

● What is the connection between the two dissections?

Dissections of a cube

You have already done some dissections of a cube on page 17.

This one cuts the cube into three parts.

◇ Make three copies of the net. Assemble them and fit them together to make a cube.

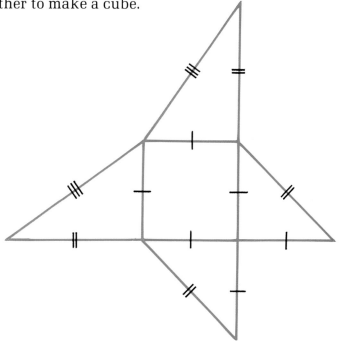

An alternative net for a square based pyramid

1. Four **congruent** triangles make the net of a square based pyramid with no base. It is easiest if you draw a circle first.

These angles must be equal. It is easier if you draw a circle first.

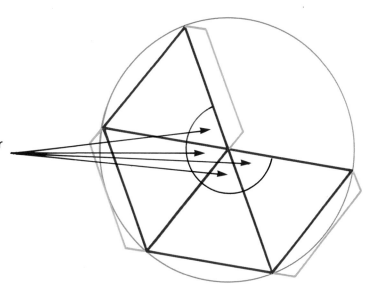

2. If you add a square to one of the triangles, that makes the base.

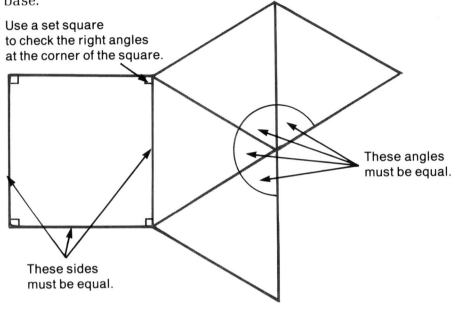

Use a set square
to check the right angles
at the corner of the square.

These angles
must be equal.

These sides
must be equal.

3. A regular octahedron has eight faces.

4. They are **equilateral** triangles.

These are the eleven possible nets for an octahedron. Notice this is the same number as the number of possible nets for a cube.

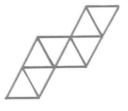

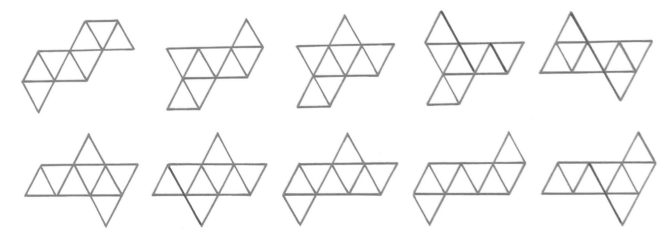

Octahedron Mobiles

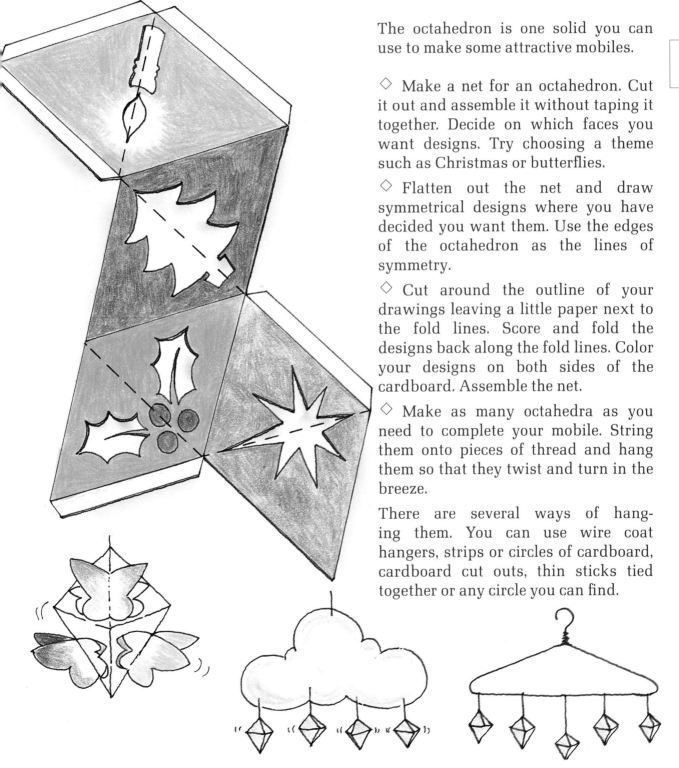

The octahedron is one solid you can use to make some attractive mobiles.

◇ Make a net for an octahedron. Cut it out and assemble it without taping it together. Decide on which faces you want designs. Try choosing a theme such as Christmas or butterflies.

◇ Flatten out the net and draw symmetrical designs where you have decided you want them. Use the edges of the octahedron as the lines of symmetry.

◇ Cut around the outline of your drawings leaving a little paper next to the fold lines. Score and fold the designs back along the fold lines. Color your designs on both sides of the cardboard. Assemble the net.

◇ Make as many octahedra as you need to complete your mobile. String them onto pieces of thread and hang them so that they twist and turn in the breeze.

There are several ways of hanging them. You can use wire coat hangers, strips or circles of cardboard, cardboard cut outs, thin sticks tied together or any circle you can find.

Answers to page 45

There are eight **convex** deltahedra. Beginning from the least number of faces, they are: the regular tetrahedron; a deltahedron with six faces, which is the same as two tetrahedra joined together; the regular octahedron; a deltahedron with ten faces, which is the same as two five-sided pyramids joined together; three deltahedra with twelve, fourteen and sixteen faces (not pictured) and the icosahedron.

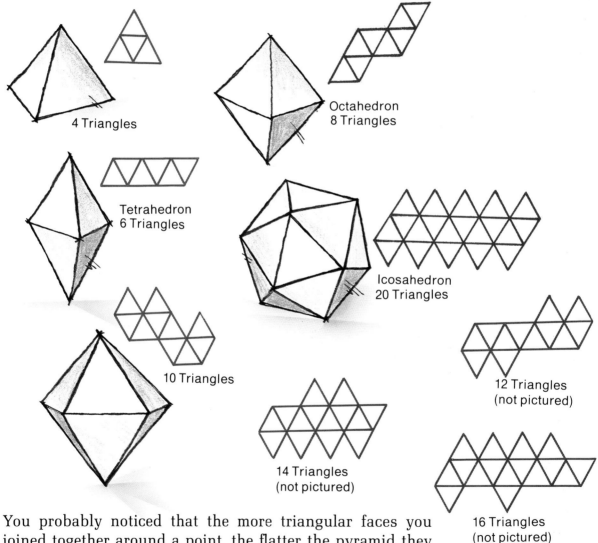

4 Triangles

Octahedron
8 Triangles

Tetrahedron
6 Triangles

Icosahedron
20 Triangles

10 Triangles

12 Triangles
(not pictured)

14 Triangles
(not pictured)

16 Triangles
(not pictured)

You probably noticed that the more triangular faces you joined together around a point, the flatter the pyramid they made. When you join six equilateral triangles around a point they lie flat and form a hexagon.

The Pentagonal Dodecahedron

The pentagonal dodecahedron is the only Platonic solid you have not yet made. You will need a piece of thin cardboard about 9 inches by 5 inches, a compass, a protractor, ruler, pencil, scissors and a rubber band.

1. On the cardboard, draw two circles each with a **radius** of 2″. Use a protractor to measure five angles of 72° at the center of the circle. (5 × 72° = 360°). Mark the angles on the **circumferences** of the circles. It is important to be as accurate as you can in measuring these five angles. Check that your last one really does measure 72°.

2. In each circle, join the five marks to form regular **pentagons**. Join each **vertex** to every other vertex. This makes another regular pentagon in the middle of the first one.

3. Join the vertices of the small pentagon and continue the lines to the edge of the large pentagon.

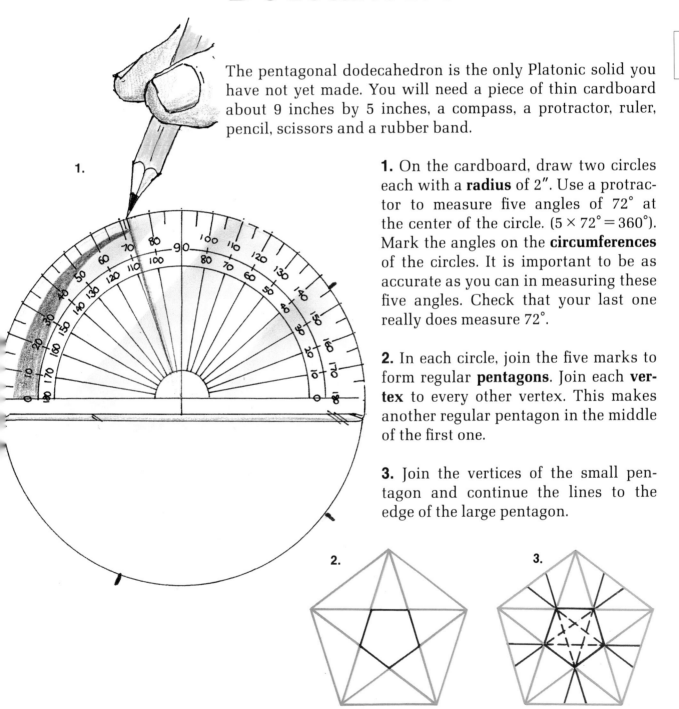

4. The shaded area is the net you need. Cut out both nets.

5. Place one net on top of the other as shown. Weave the rubber band around the two pieces with one hand and use the other to keep the pieces flat. When the band is all the way around, release the two pieces and they erect themselves into a dodecahedron.

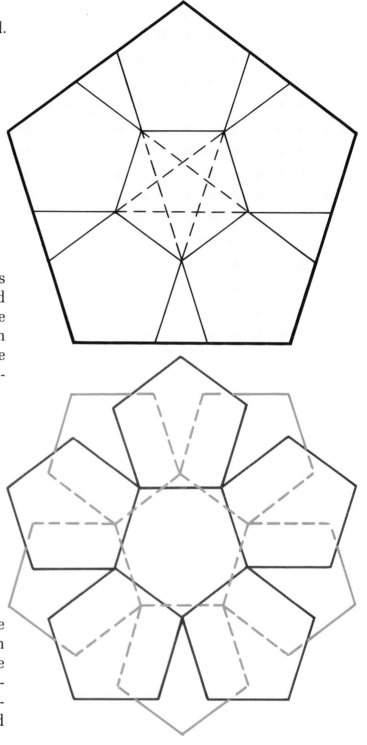

Since the dodecahedron has twelve faces, you can use it to make an unusual calendar. It is better to use tabs and glue instead of tape to construct it. You can also make an attractive paperweight by decorating it and filling it with sand.

Stellations

You can make some very attractive star-shaped polyhedra by fastening pyramids onto the faces of polyhedra. They are called stellated polyhedra because "stella" is the Latin word for "star."

You can experiment with any polyhedra and any pyramids, but only some combinations will produce stars with regular patterns.

The stellated dodecahedron

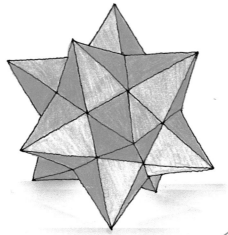

The stellated dodecahedron is made from pyramids attached to a regular dodecahedron.

This is the net you need for the pyramids. The short edge of each triangle needs to be the same length as the edge of your dodecahedron.

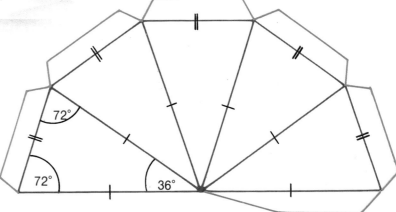

● **1.** How many pyramids must you make?

The stellated icosahedron

The base of the model is a regular icosahedron. The pyramids have three triangular faces with the same angles as the triangles for the stellated dodecahedron. Look back at page 50.

- **2.** How many pyramids do you need?

- **3.** What do you have to remember about the length of the short side of the triangles?

The stella octangula

You can make this by first making an octahedron and then attaching a **regular tetrahedron** to each of its faces.

- **4.** What is the connection between the net for the octahedron and the net for each regular tetrahedron?

A stellated cube

Make the cross-shaped net for a cube. Make the nets for the square based pyramids that fit on the faces of the cube. The square bases of the pyramids must be the same size as the faces of the cube.

Assemble the solid.

● **1.** What is the name of the solid you make when you fold up the model so that the pyramids are on the inside of it?

● **2.** What is the solid called when the pyramids are on the outside?

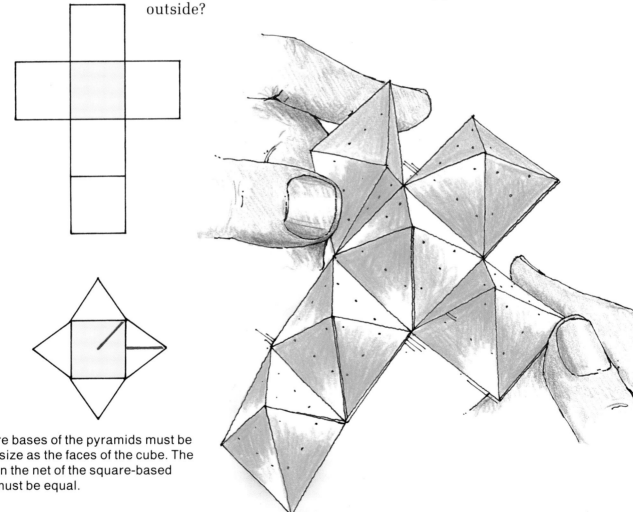

The square bases of the pyramids must be the same size as the faces of the cube. The red lines in the net of the square-based pyramid must be equal.

Cross Sections

We have already seen that a **perpendicular** cross section of a **prism** is the same shape as its end faces (page 18).

- **1.** Can you match the cross sections to the solids?

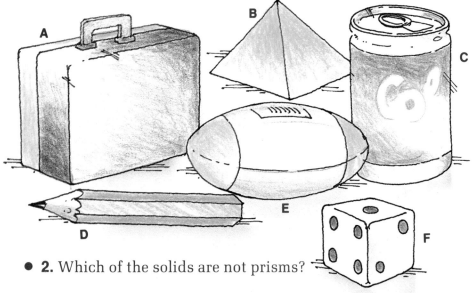

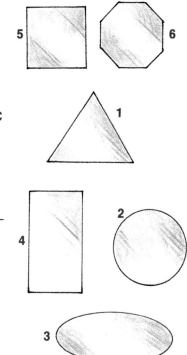

- **2.** Which of the solids are not prisms?

Investigation

- **a)** If you make a series of cross sections **parallel** to the base of a cone, what shape are they?
- **b)** What happens the higher up the cone you go?
- **c)** What shapes can you make with cross sections that are perpendicular to the base?
- **d)** What other shapes can you make with cross sections of a cone?

You may find it helpful to make a cone from modeling clay and slice it up.

◇ Investigate making cross sections with other solids.

Schlegel Diagrams

A German mathematician named Schlegel invented a way of drawing solids. You have to imagine that the front face of the solid is removed and that the solid is is stretched out until it is flat.

A cube works like this.

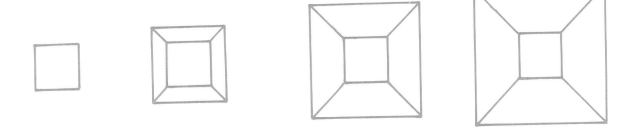

● **1.** Try to identify these solids from their Schlegel diagrams.

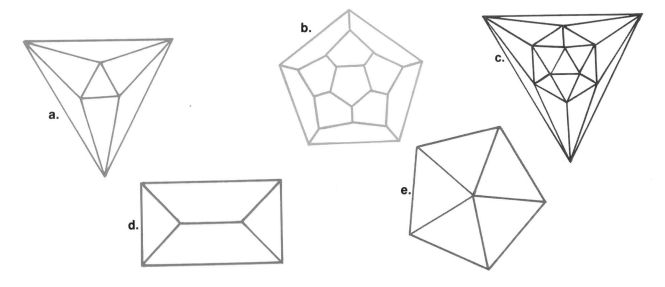

● **2.** Draw a Schlegel diagram of a tetrahedron.

58

Glossary

circumference the boundary of a circle or the distance around it

congruent the same shape and size

convex a convex polyhedron is one in which the line joining any two points on its surface lies completely inside the polyhedron

cube a solid with six square faces

cuboid a solid with six rectangular faces

deltahedron a polyhedron whose faces are all equilateral triangles

dodecahedron a polyhedron with twelve faces; the faces of a regular dodecahedron are regular pentagons

edge an edge of a solid is the boundary of a face

equilateral triangle a triangle with three equal sides; it has three angles of 60°

face a surface of a solid which is bounded by edges

factor a factor of a number divides it exactly with no remainder; 1, 2, 3, 4, 6 and 12 are all factors of 12

hexagon a six-sided shape

hexomino a pattern of six squares joined edge to edge

icosahedron a polyhedron with twenty faces

isosceles an isosceles triangle has two sides of the same length; it also has two angles of the same size

net a two-dimensional pattern for making a three-dimensional solid

octahedron a solid with eight triangular faces; a regular octahedron has equilateral triangular faces

parallel parallel lines always remain the same distance apart; railway tracks are made of a pair of parallel rails

parallelogram a four-sided shape with two pairs of parallel sides

pentagon a five-sided shape

pentomino a pattern of five squares joined edge to edge

perpendicular two faces or edges are perpndicular when they are at right angles to each other

polyhedron a solid whose faces are all flat

power the number of times a number is multiplied by itself; 3^4 means $3 \times 3 \times 3 \times 3 = 81$

prism a solid whose two parallel ends are the same

radius the distance from the center to the edge of a circle

rectangle a shape with four straight sides and four right angles

reflection a mirror image; the result of flipping over a solid, shape or pattern

regular in a regular polyhedron, all the faces, edges and vertices are the same

rhombus a four-sided shape with equal sides; a square is a special rhombus – it has right angles

right angle a quarter turn; 90°

rotation the result of turning a solid, shape or pattern around

set square a mathematical instrument for measuring right angles and drawing parallel lines

tetrahedron a pyramid with four triangular faces; a regular tetrahedron has equilateral triangular faces

vertex the point where two or more edges meet

Answers

Page 7
See pages 8-9
Page 10
See page 14
Page 11
1. The open box has five faces.
2. They are squares.
3. The open box has twelve edges.
4. Three edges meet at each vertex.
5. There are eight vertices.
Page 12
1. A cube has six faces.
2. A cuboid has eight vertices.
3. Two faces meet at each edge of a cube.
4. Three edges meet at each vertex of a cube.
5. A cuboid has twelve edges.
Page 13
Investigation – see page 16
Challenge – see page 17
Page 15
1, **6**, **8** and **10** make open boxes with a funny face on the bottom.
Page 17
See pages 20-21
Page 18
1. Yes, cuboids are prisms.
Page 19
2. The net of a cylinder is a rectangle and two circles.
Investigation – a short fat cylinder holds more than a tall thin one.
Page 22
See page 27
Page 24
See page 28

Page 26
Samantha's puzzle – see page 31
Evan's puzzle – see page 38
Page 28
See page 34
Page 29
See page 30
Page 30
The rhombic dodecahedron is not a regular polyhedron because not all the vertices are the same. Some have three edges meeting, others have four.
Page 33
1. A sphere has one face.
2. The only edge it has is its outer boundary.
3. A sphere has no vertices.
4. The cross section is always a circle – try it by cutting an orange.
5. A sphere is not a polyhedron.
Page 34
See page 37
Page 35
These are the squares that must be colored.

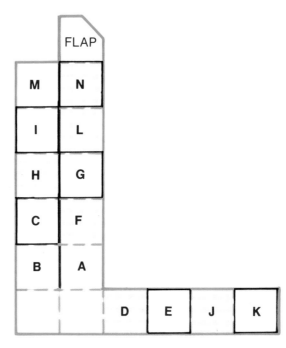

Page 36

1. and 2. A tetrahedron has four triangular faces.
3. It has six edges.
4. It has four vertices.
5. Three edges meet at each vertex.
6. No, Albert ant could not walk around all the edges without retracing his steps.

Page 37

1. 8 is the smallest number of small cubes that can be joined together to make a larger cube.
2. See page 38

Page 38

These are some of the patterns in the table.

There are always eight faces with three sides painted.

The number of cubes with two faces painted is always a **factor** of 12. If you subtract 2 from the number of cubes on one edge and multiply by 12, you get the number of cubes with two faces painted.

The number of cubes with one face painted is always a factor of 6. If you subtract 2 from the number of cubes on one edge, multiply the result by itself and then multiply by 6, you get the number of cubes with one face painted.

To find the number of cubes with no faces painted, subtract 2 from the number of cubes on one edge and multiply the result by itself 3 times. This is the same as taking away the sum of the painted cubes from the total number of cubes.

For a cube with 100 cubes along each edge:
Painted faces

3	2	1	0
8	98×12	$98 \times 98 \times 6$	98^3
8	1,176	57,624	941,192

There are 1,000,000 small cubes in a $100 \times 100 \times 100$ cube, so we can total the results in the table as a check.

$$8 + 1,176 + 57,624 + 941,192 = 1,000,000$$

Page 39

1. Four faces are hidden.
2. One rule is to multiply the number of cubes by 3 and subtract 2 from the result.
3. For 20 cubes, the number of faces hidden
$$= (20 \times 3) - 2$$
$$= 60 - 2$$
$$= 58$$

Page 40

See page 44

Page 41

The fifth face is a square. Net on page 42
Challenge – See page 42
Yes, it is possible to travel along all the edges without going over an edge more than once. This is one way.

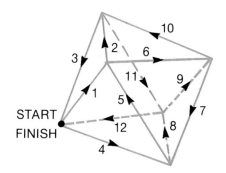

Page 42

1. The triangles are **isosceles**.
2. Equilateral triangles work as well.
3. Do not make the four angles congruent.

Page 43

1. See page 47.
2-5. and investigation – See page 48.

Page 44

Puzzle answer a square whose diagonal is a wee bit larger than 2″. If it is exactly 2″ the tetrahedron will not pass through.

Page 45
See page 50

Page 46
Two of the second set of solids joined together make one of the first pair of solids.

Page 53
1. You need twelve pyramids.

Page 54
2. You need twenty pyramids.

3. The length of the short side of the triangles must be the same length as the edges of the icosahedron.

4. The tetrahedron net is made from four equilateral triangles of the same size as the faces of the octahedron.

Page 55
1. A cube.

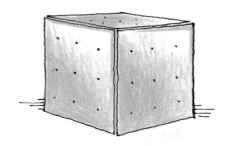

2. A rhombic dodecahedron.

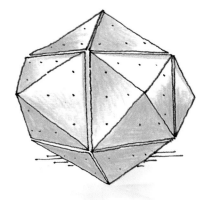

Page 56
1. A matches **4**
B matches **1**
C matches **2**
D matches **6**
E matches **3**
F matches **5**

2. The only true prism is **F**.

Investigation
a) circular
b) the circles decrease in radius until they shrink to a point
c) parabolas
d) ovals

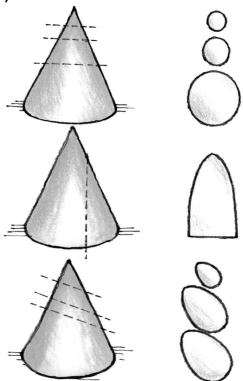

Page 57
1. a) octahedron
b) pentagonal dodecahedron
c) icosahedron
d) triangular based prism
e) five sided pyramid

2.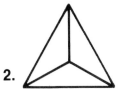

Index